Bookkeeping & Accounting With Quickbooks Online

SADANAND PUJARI

Published by SADANAND PUJARI, 2023.

Table of Contents

Copyright

Copyright © 2023 by **SADANAND PUJARI**

Bookkeeping & Accounting With Quickbooks Online

First Edition: Dec 2023

Book Design by **SADANAND PUJARI**

About

Learn quickbooks online as quickly as possible, perfect for beginners. Learn the basics and start using quickbooks online immediately. Lots of examples for you to practice

QuickBooks Online is one of the most popular bookkeeping & accounting software. In this Book I will show you how to do bookkeeping & accounting in QuickBooks Online.

If you find traditional bookkeeping textbooks and classes boring and confusing, then this Book is perfect for you because I explain everything in plain simple language that's easy to understand and fun to learn.

In fact, many students have told me this is a great Book and easy to understand.

Bookkeeping Project Outline and Plan

Within the bookkeeping project outline and a plan chapter of the Book will go over the outline of the project. We will be discussing whether we are a business owner ourselves who wants a simple method, a cash basis method for entering information into quick books or a bookkeeping business.

We'll discuss it from the standpoint of a bookkeeping business. But the same principles apply if we are a business and want a cash basis system. We will talk about the type of businesses where this system will work best in a more of a cash basis system and some of the challenges with a system like this and we'll discuss what we'll do to overcome some of those challenges and discuss them later on in the Book will outline the project of the Book and what we'll be doing in later chapters of the Book.

Outline Of Standard Client Or Business

In this chapter we will take a look at the type of clients and the type Of Book Keeping system for which our system will work well for. In other words we're putting together a very systematic bookkeeping system and it will work well for certain types of customers and certain types of needs. So whether we are a business that is thinking about implementing an accounting system such as this or a bookkeeping business that wants to pick up clients we need to understand the types of clients that we want to pick up.

Clearly we want to pick up types of clients that have integrity that we're going to work well with. We're going to get paid from that perspective. We also want to know what types of clients we want to pick up in terms of their needs so that we can specialize what we do to a specific client and that's what we're doing within bookkeeping, even accounting within bookkeeping. We've got to trim our needs down. What we do is down to specifics so we can specialize and differentiate in this way. This is one way to differentiate by doing a specific type Of Book Keeping. Who are we going to apply this bookkeeping for?

What type of clients are we looking for when we're using this type Of Book Keeping system? If we want to vary it from that system if and when do we want to do that. These are questions we need to know and understand as we go through our bookkeeping process. First we wanted to find what we do and what type of client would fit well for what we do. And for this case we're going to be talking about small businesses because we will be offering a cash basis service. So what we're gonna do is bookkeeping specific bookkeeping on a cash basis in a simplistic type of way.

Getting the information directly from the bank statement in a cash basis format and that will typically work for smaller businesses who have specific needs oftentimes to compile the information in a format that can be useful for end of the year needs such as tax preparation and financial statements. We'll talk more about what this includes and in defining what it is we do and what type of clients we work with. We also need to define what we do not do and what types of clients we were not going to take on so that we can focus in on our specialty so areas to consider are gonna be the areas that are kind of in between we want to think about such as inventory typically where we're not taking on inventory in this type of system because if we want a full service tracking of inventory that's going to add a level of complexity.

So we'll talk about different ways that we can think about inventory we may want to work with a small client for inventory but if we take on our client that has inventory we need to be straightforward with what types of services we're going to provide in terms of tracking that inventory how we're going to deal with that inventory otherwise we may just want to not be working with customers who have a significant need to track inventory and work with more types of clients that just have service type industries because those lend themselves to a straight cash basis format more easily. So we will actually work on a problem where we will have inventory involved so you can see the kind of complications that you may run into with inventory in the system and decide for yourself if you want to include inventory.

Do you want to just work with customers that don't have that inventory type needed? Payroll is another issue that we want to consider whether the customer has payroll or not. Do we want to work with the types of clients that are sole proprietors and don't have any payroll needs they're just going to be sole proprietors and just need the needs for the financial statements. Basically the profit loss or income statement or if they do have payroll. How are we going to deal with payroll? Do we want to have an outside service dealing with payroll.

Do we want to enter the payroll ourselves and take on that level of complexity? We will include payroll just so we can see some of the complications with payrolls and some of the options that we have with payroll. However if we're starting out we might want to consider taking on small customers that don't have the payroll needs or we don't need to take on the payroll needs. And again we'll look at some other options that we can use to deal with payroll. We also want to be clear on what it is we do not do in this system. So in our system we're looking at here we're not going to be doing a full service accrual bookkeeping.

We'll talk about what that is. What we are doing is a cash basis bookkeeping based on the information that is in the bank. We'll take a look at more detail of what those differences are. We're not going to be doing tax preparation and you can think about doing tax preparation but we're going to argue here that we're just doing bookkeeping at this point not tax preparation we'll discuss why that can be beneficial in some cases for bookkeeping we're not doing financial state with preparation meaning we're not doing audits of financial statements or compilations or reviews we're just basically providing the reports necessary. We'll talk more about that full service payroll.

We're typically not going to be doing the service payroll process and we'll think about some workarounds for dealing with payroll as well so let's get into a little bit more detail about these items. Full service accrual bookkeeping full service accrual bookkeeping means that we're going to be tracking things like accounts receivable and accounts payable. We're going to be entering invoices, we're going to be entering bills, we're going to be entering the data as it happens throughout the time period in our system we're proposing here. We're not doing that. What we're really doing is taking the information that's cleared from the bank already and entering that data into the system. And that means we have no accounts receivable. That means we have no revenue recognition principle; we're not recognizing revenue when the work is done as we'd be done under an accrual method. But when it cleared the bank that's when we're going to recognize revenue. So it's not a full service system in that format.

We're just doing the data input really on from the bank statements. We're also not doing a matching principle meaning we're not entering the expenses when they happen. We're entering the expenses when they cleared the bank. Now there will be some exceptions if we see like large transactions and whatnot we're going to have to do some accrual type concepts meaning for example if we paid cash for equipment we'll put that on as an acid and if we took out a loan or something like that we'll have to deal with some accounts that will be kind of more accrual related but we're not going through the full process and the major things that we will notice on the balance sheet is that we're not invoicing people we're not tracking accounts receivable.

We're not eating bills and we're not tracking accounts payable. So again if a company really needs that we'll discuss a little bit how they can track the accounts receivable out you know in our system using a system like this. However if a customer needs the system in order to process invoices like bills from that company file and send those out. That's not what we're really doing, we're just entering the data into the system. In our case if the company wants to track outstanding payables who is owed money to. That's not what we are really doing. Either we're just basically putting the bills that have been paid into the system. So it's important when we discuss with clients what it is we're proposing to do here and what we're not doing.

Tax preparation is also something I wouldn't recommend doing in this type of format. So taxes are like income taxes at the end of the year Form 10 40 income taxes. If you were to take on income taxes it could be a revenue stream for income tax but it's also something that can get complicated fairly quickly because once we start doing taxes we'll have the business taxes and then we'll have the personal taxes. And if you do not do the taxes it could be beneficial for bookkeepers because then you can work with CPA firms and other accounting firms that do taxes but don't want to do as much of the data entry type Of Book Keeping process and they're more than willing to work with bookkeepers that want to pick that up. And so you can, it's a lot.

We'll talk a little bit more about networking and who you can work with. And it's a lot easier to set up a system that we will be proposing if we can work with tax preparers and accounting firms and CPA firms. They can help with the end of the period adjustments help with things like tax preparation help with things like payroll help with things like into the period adjustments. So we're going to be actually dependent on those things to be done by things like accounting firms under a system like this and it's easier to work with them if they don't think that we're competing on the areas that they see as their major revenue source. So if we don't compete on the tax side but do the bookkeeping and use them for the tax side we have a very good type of relationship that could build on a business side of things. So that's why under this type of system we're proposing here whether it be our books or whether it be where we have taken on clients that we do not do the tax preparation and work with somebody the tax preparer either someone that we propose or whatever tax preparer the client would like us to work with.

But it'd be nice for us to build a relationship with the tax preparers because we can feed each other in terms of clients and working and being able to work more efficiently and all that financial statement preparation. What we will do in our system, which is our main goal for the small companies, is often to make basically an income statement at the end of the year that can be used to help in the year processing including including the tax return. So that's usually what the data entry is often needed for for small companies. They want to track what they're doing. They want to make sure that they're getting the financial statement at least compiled from the bank and that information then being put into such a format that can't be used for the tax preparation.

So although we're making reports such as a profit loss and balance sheet possibly we're focusing on more of the profit and loss. We're not really reviewing and we're not putting any opinion on those. We're not saying that these are correct in our opinion as a format of a review or an attestation type of format. We're just entering the data and giving reports for that data if they need a review such as for a loan. If you needed to have a loan or something like that the bank may want some type of opinion on the financial statements and for that again we'd want to work with the CPA firm so we would want to work with an accounting firm so that they can take that information and then process it to give their opinion on that information. That's not what we do here.

We're just putting the data into the system to process the reports for it. It's important to be clear about that with with the clients and let the clients know that hey this is what we're entering into into the system doesn't mean that we're we're giving our assurance in it as would be the case basically for financial statement preparation and we'll talk a little bit more about making that clear in terms of an engagement letter when we've talked about putting together an engagement letter in terms of what we do and what we're not doing. Full service payroll office is also something that I would recommend. Under this system we're not not to take on the full service payroll and work with clients either that are sole proprietors that don't have the payroll or that have a fairly limited payroll and if they have limited payroll we may want we could.

One option is to look at the payroll within the system and see if we want to take that on or another option would be to work with the CPA firm or payroll professionals. There's a lot of companies that just do payroll and again that could be a very good relationship. Payroll is another area that could be a lot of liability in place and it can get complex really quick even with very few employees. Payroll can start to get somewhat complex and therefore it may be worthwhile for us to start working with a payroll company that will basically take on those needs outside of our system. And we then we'll just enter the payroll checks into the system from what they give us so that we can still be on a cash basis just entering the data on a very simplified cash basis and the payroll can be taken care of by payroll professionals and we can get any adjusting entries needed at the end of the time period for tax preparation as we work with the CPA firm.

So our goal here is to make things basically as simple as possible for an easy bookkeeping process whether it be us for simplified clients or us in terms of our own books and work with other professionals for those specialized needs in order to make that happen. So to do that then we need to define exactly what it is we do exactly what we're looking for the others to do and then we can define how to work with that system and put together a system that's very efficient in that format.

Note what payroll involves we have to not only pay the employees and track that but we have to take withholdings for federal as is the U.S. withholding federal income tax social security medicare state taxes if there's multiple states or regions very that gets very complex very quickly so we want to you know probably have hope that if we're not aware of the state taxes that we're in then then again that's another area we would probably want to stay away from unless we're we're really getting like the full service type of front forward form our software but it's probably something we want to work with someone else for we have to pay the payroll taxes to to the Fed or the state or the client's going to have to have that system to determine how much to pay to the Fed or the state and within the nine forties in the 940 once quarterlies and yearly forums as well as state forms would need to be generated. So even with a few employees this could start to get fairly complex to process and may be worthwhile under a simplified system for us to just work with it with another professional to basically take on the payroll.

Outline Of Book Keeping Process

In this chapter we will take a look at the outline of the bookkeeping process. We are proposing more of a cash basis bookkeeping process. We will outline this as if we are a bookkeeping business with multiple clients. However this information does apply as well if we are working on our own business file. The format of how we would set up the information on more of a cash basis setting will be the same. Even if we're just working on our own books, we'll also be talking about some factors.

If we had multiple clients as we discussed through this we might have multiple clients that we are specializing in with one type of system and we're looking for that type of client that we can then specialize in within this type of system of this type of system being more of a cash basis type of system. First of all, what does that mean? What is a cash basis type system? We can think of accounting as a kind of spectrum from a cash basis to an accrual basis and we could think of those two ends at the end of the spectrum and many businesses actually operate somewhere in between.

More on the side of a cash basis or more on the side of an accrual basis and those two are basically the extremes of the spectrum. What we're thinking about here is being more on the side of the cash bases cookbooks Of course allows us the capability to do more accrual accounting the more accrual accounting we have means that we're going to have more detail with the accounting. It's typically better to typically think of more information to have accrual accounting. However Of course the cash accounting is something that will typically be easier. It'll be easier for us to input. It typically takes less time to input that information and we could be much more reliant on something like the bank statement which is actually in essence a third party bank providing the bookkeeping for us.

Everything that goes through the bank has a record for us. So a cash basis system would be to just in essence take that bank statement and put it into the bookkeeping system. The benefit of this system is it will be easier and faster to do but we also need to know when it would apply, what type of companies it would apply for and there's certain types of industries that there's going to be more of a problem for. For example if we're in an industry that really wants to track the accounts receivable very closely within the quick book system it's going to be more difficult to apply a system that's basically dependent on a cash basis dependent on the bank statement or if we have a type of company that has a lot of inventory it may be something that will be more difficult to apply just a cash basis system in that format.

So we need to consider as we think about the types of clients a format like this would work for what types of clients have the needs that this system would be best for and those will typically be service based business or businesses that have inventory that track that inventory in some place and want to in essence track it outside of the system possibly in Excel or something like that so that we can this enter and depend on the bank statement as the data input point. And as we do so we'll create the financial statements from the data, the financial transactions and the financial data on a cash basis from the bank statement.

The basic process will be to start new Quickbooks files. We started a quick books online file and we could start that with our accounting dashboard. We'll talk about a couple of different options for setting up the QuickBooks Online file. Once it's set up we want to create a chart of accounts based on the industry and Quickbooks helps us to do that. We'll put in the industry QuickBooks will help us to create a chart of accounts. It's usually pretty good at that. That'll be a great starting point for us to then add accounts or delete accounts that we either need or don't need in the future. Then we'll enter transactions each month from the bank statement.

Now we could use bank feeds to do this but either way we think about it whether we use bank feeds or whether we enter simply from the bank statement that's provided to us by the client or if it's our business our bank statement. It's in essence the same system we're talking about here because we're taking that data directly from the bank and basically being completely dependent on that rather than us entering the data first and then having the bank basically double check it. So in essence we're basically depending on the bank as our primary source of the bookkeeping information they are doing the books in instead of us verifying with them as a second outside reporter of the books which is a great tool.

We are in essence depending on them to give us their books their information on a cash basis that will enter into the system either with bank feeds or just straight into the register and then we'll do the bank reconciliation the bank reconciliation is still something we really want to do but it won't give the same kind of verification. Note that if we did the full accounting process we would be doing the bookkeeping on our own on our own. Then the bank would also be clearing this information from the bank statement. The bank reconciliation would then be a check that an outside set Of courses matches our set Of courses which were made separately in this case Of course were dependent on the bank completely to enter the data into the system. So the bank reconciliation doesn't give the same kind of verification but it still gives some verification and in essence it gives verification that we have entered the data properly.

In other words we're gonna take the transactions directly from the bank statement, enter it directly into the system and then we'll double check with the bank reconciliation that we've entered that data from the bank exactly as it appears on the bank statement. That's what the bank reconciliation will do. It'll still be useful won't give the same type of verification it's important to note that the internal control for the bank reconciliation here isn't quite the same but it's still unnecessary internal control we should do and then we want to provide monthly reports to the clients so we then give the reports to the clients we can print them out give them in the format of a PDf we Of course from the online version can give clients access to the file as well so they can go in and print any reports they want.

However under the system we're provoked. We are proposing here. We're trying to keep the bookkeeping separate so we don't typically want the client entering data into the system. We're proposing basically a cash basis system where we are entering all the data directly from the bank statement as opposed to a system where we would be just basically helping the data input process that the client would be entering. So under this system we were basically saying we have one data input process.

We're taking it from the bank statement and we have one person in control of that whether it be the bookkeeper of the owner of the business and not in essence a management process where the client is entering data and then we're going to enter data to mix things up for the most part normally. So what we want to do is say hey this is what we're proposing here. We're proposing to do the bank statements directly from or into the data directly from the bank statements to do all the data input process. You have complete control of the data file is yours you have access to it however we would like to basically be in control of the data input for it and then so that will manage the data input as best we can and then provide you with the reports and you can take a look and print that your own reports from the system we would advise not to be entering data without letting us know into the quick buck system and that'll give assurance to the client as well because if they leave if they want to go somewhere else it's their data file they can take it and leave.

This is just for logistics purposes that we have one person basically entering the data and that's going to be the best way to keep the data as clean as possible. When we start a new quick books file we'll do it in quick books online so we'll have to pay for that new QuickBooks file. We'll have to set up the new QuickBooks file. Once we do that we'll just need basically the client name and industry and that'll be enough to get us up and running with the new QuickBooks file if we have multiple clients we're gonna want to be using QuickBooks accountants and that give us our own little dashboard if we use Quickbooks accountant and it'll basically have our clients down here so the client can have their basically their log in and we can have our log in here and it'll give us access to go into the client data as well as the client having their own access on their side of the data. So a dashboard like this helps us basically to manage our clients. It may also help us to provide discounts for services for clients as well.

So we want to get if we have multiple clients the QuickBooks accountant if it's just our file Of course if we're doing this for our own company file then we don't typically need the quick books accounting we would just be running our one file we would have the data input to get into it. The difference Of course here being that if we have multiple files we can get into multiple files and if you manage it with you want the client to be in the file and we want to be in the file as well. This allows for basically that access and you can also basically have a team here that you can assign different individuals, different bookkeeping people within your team to have access to the file as well and be able to manage that so you can delegate more easily within a system such as this.

Once we set up the industry, cookbooks will actually give us a chart of accounts which is great so cookbooks will start off with a chart of accounts and we're all basically up and running. Ready to go with that chart of accounts we can then basically enter the data if that data be something from a client that already has business data that we need to enter or if it's a new client and we're going to start from scratch here we are in essence good to go at that point we will need to make some adjustments Of course to the chart of accounts if they already have a chart of accounts we're going have to we can make some adjustments and take a look at the chart of accounts that they have from their prior industry and see if we want to keep it or not and see how we want to manage that information going forward if it's a new company then the chart of accounts is really usually a good place to start because it is a standard chartered accountant is based on industry standards.

Next thing we're going to do is put the information into quick books based on the bank statement. So we'll ask for big statements from the client. We'll use those to enter the data into the system. Now if the client would like us to access their bank and give us the bank feeds and that would mean they would have to give us the banking information so that we can link to the bank. That would be great because then we would have the automatic link to the grant to the bank and we can download or if not if we don't want that system or they don't want to give us the bank linked directly into quick books then we could just take the same type of system to take the bank statements and entered into quick books the way we're setting up the system is similar either way here because we're really being dependent just on the bank. So either way we're basically saying hey whatever goes through the bank that's what's going to go into the quick buck system. And remember what that doesn't.

What that means is we're not tracking things that don't go through the bank. So we're not putting things like accounts receivable accounts payable accrual type of transactions aren't being tracked under this system. If there's people that owe the company money or something like that, accounts receivable that the client's going to have to track that on their own outside of the system or we'll have to put a work around into the system we are using to work with this. So we really want to emphasize that when we discuss this with clients we're saying hey this is a cash based system.

We're going to take the info you really need to make sure that your bank statement has all the information going through it make sure that you're using a bank statement that is your business account that has all the transactions going through it and then we'll be able to take that bank statement and will enter that into the system. Also note that it's not good enough typically to have just a running balance of the accounts meaning you don't just want to get a print out of any of the bank transactions over a certain time period. We want to have a beginning Palin's and an Indian balance because that helps us to enter the data reconcile the data make sure that we're not missing transactions makes sure that we're not duplicating transactions if we don't have the cut off the standard cutoffs here then we can't reconcile as easily and we're not we're not giving us that check of not reconciling and we're not as sure if we if we didn't duplicate a transaction or if we didn't miss some transactions then we will do the bank reconciliation.

Remember that the bank reconciliation will just be a verification. In essence, we took this stuff directly from the bank statement and entered it directly into quick books correctly. There's not going to be any outstanding checks or outstanding deposits as we would assume there to be. If we were doing a full service bookkeeping system because we just took this information directly from the bank statement and put it into the system outstanding checks outstanding deposits would result from us entering the data as we write the checks which we're not doing here because we're not we're not writing the checks in the system we're waiting until they clear to record them in the system. So that means that there's not going to be outstanding checks and outstanding deposits because we're not entering the data as it happens.

We're entering the data from the bank statement after it's cleared. And so just be aware of that. However the bank reconciliation is still important because it gives us that verification that we double checks that we enter the data correctly into the quick buck system then we provide monthly reports to the clients which will include the balance sheet and the profit loss in any other report that we think will be necessary at that time the balance sheet and a profit loss Of course are kind of like the minimum reports that we will have.

We'll also provide the client with the information that they can go in and print any reports that they want at any given time. But it's probably good practice though to give them in a PDL format or some other format. The balance sheet and the income statement give a batch of the reports at the end of each month to just basically say hey here's the information we're working for year. Here's the balance sheet, here's the profit loss, probably the bank reconciliation as well. And this will give a verification to the clients that we're still working on this will still go and notice that the clients are probably not as concerned with the monthly statements because they're doing their business they're not probably as concerned with what they really want.

Most likely under a system if it's a cash basis system a smaller client is the year end information but the monthly information well presented lets the client know hey we're here for you still go on we'll be here at the end of the year the data is being compiled it'll be ready for you when you have the taxes and whatnot and you got to put all the information you got put together at the end of the year that that would be the standard system we are proposing but there could be some alternative cases for example if we had a company file in our own business or if we had client company files where we had to enter year end information and we don't have any information for the entire year we have multiple months of information that hasn't been entered then we might have to enter multiple months of information at that point in time and then hopefully going forward after we do that we can convince ourselves that or others to do that on a monthly basis and go back to the other system.

But we might have to enter multiple months at the start point of the bookkeeping service. So in that case Of course we would then enter the multiple months in the same system we would want to get the bank statements for multiple months. We would just take those bank statements and enter all the data directly from the bank statement. We would process the bank reconciliations on a monthly basis to verify that we're entering that data improperly. And then we can provide the monthly reports to the client as well as enter all that data at one time. So this is one method. This is one way for example if we're at the end of the year and we don't have all the information that we can compile this information using the bank statements into the quick book system and then hopefully use that information Of course then to create the financial statements the profit loss oftentimes the major statement that would be necessary front for a small business to then process the tax returns.

One of the nice things about using cookbooks online is that we can easily provide access to the client files. So whether it be our file if it's our business file we're entering in the data then we can provide that information to say our accountant or tax preparer at the end of the year fairly easily in it and the accountant or tax preparer may have cookbooks accountant and therefore be able to access the data without using the same data input the same password and whatnot to access that file if we're the bookkeeper then we can also provide the information to the client as well.

The client could have their own log in information and we can use a cookbook accountant to manage our client information that way as well as give them the information and access to someone else that would be necessary to process the information like a tax preparer. At the end of the year as well. Note however that as we do this we do want to emphasize that although the client has access to it although it's the client's file and if they want to leave or something happens or if they want to print reports all there for the client we do want to try to keep this the data input separate so that we are just entering the data from the bank statement. So we don't muddy any up.

So we just basically want to be us on the data input side but providing the access to the file to the client so generally they can process their reports and just feel comfortable that it is their file and then be able to also provide that file to the accountant at the end of the year or the tax preparer at the end of the year.

Network With Other Professionals

In this chapter we will discuss networking opportunities for the system that we are proposing for bookkeeping. In other words whether they be our books or whether we are a bookkeeping company that has clients that we are providing bookkeeping for. It's a good idea to have some of these networks involved to help us with the components of the bookkeeping process areas that we will need support.

Typically will include the areas of taxation, the area of adjusting entries, these beard periods and adjusting. Entries will go into more detail in these in a second. The area of financial statement preparation and payroll. So let's first just talk about taxes. Typically if we're doing the bookkeeping whether it be our sales or if we have a bookkeeping business oftentimes it's useful. Under this system I'm proposing to keep the taxes separate and if we do that then we can network with tax professionals to help us out with the tax component. And that's a really good network because then we're not competing with each other for that component and we can then do what we do and we can work with other tax professionals and be able to refer to each other, know how each other works and be able to specialize in that format for taxation.

Who could we work with for taxation? Well we could work with an accounting firm or a CPA firm. And if we work with an accounting firm or CPA firm that's often really useful because not only will that help with taxation but it will typically help with some of the other things we will need at the end of the year.

If we are working with small clients or if we are a small business then we may only need taxation at the end of the year. We might not need other types of services from a full service CPA firm or accounting firm but we may need some in the future. And if we're a bookkeeping bookkeeping business then we're going to probably run into clients now and again that's going to need more than possibly just tax preparation.

We can also work with enrolled agents that specialize just in tax preparation. Again if we work with on a roll and enrolled agent firms that just basically do tax preparation that's really helpful for that component tax preparation but they may not have as much flexibility with the different types of taxes that may be involved. And so the complexity of taxes may be a higher level of complexity at a CPA firm or accounting firm that does taxation as opposed to an unreal agent. However if we're working with small businesses then an enrolled agent would probably be sufficient to pick up the tax preparation. What an enrolled agent may not do as well is some of the other things that we'll talk about shortly.

The adjusting entries being one of them. So the adjusting entries are things that we do at the end of the period and the way we're gonna propose putting together our bookkeeping system is on a cash basis. And as such it's very useful for us to be able to work with somebody to make periodic judgments so that we can say hey this is what we're doing. We're going to define what we're doing in this very defined way and we can list out things that we're not going to do and depend on the period and adjustments for the tax preparation at the end of the year and we'll discuss more of that when we go through the accounting problem here. Once we start entering data but if we have a CPA firm or accounting firm that we can rely on that can be a really good relationship because we can basically say hey when it comes to these areas when it comes to things like payroll when it comes to this type of loan documentation that a loan was taken out.

How are we going to amortize the loan payments or insurance when they have insurance and they paid for an entire year's worth of insurance. These types of things we can work out a nice easy system so that we can go through our just bookkeeping process enter that data just as we would from the bank statement and you and help and tell the CPA firm or the accounting firm what we've done and then give them the adjustments to the documentation to make any adjustments that would be necessary for the tax preparation at the end of the year. That kind of thing is something that a CPA firm may be more able to do and it will provide that separation between the bookkeeping process and the adjusting entries that might be necessary and not as easy to do with an in an enrolled agent which may not be able to see that distinction or how that kind of separation could work quite as easily or maybe you can find one that could but just be aware of that process. And we'll talk more about that as we start to enter the data into the system. What type of things can we set up to make that differentiation?

Financial Statement preparation. Now we are compiling data here. That's what we're doing Of course and the system is going to prepare. Kind of like financial statements, the profit loss and balance sheet. But note that this is different from us doing audited financial statements. So what we're doing is compounding the situation the statement probably for a year in information for personal information for the company and probably for tax preparation that and then give for tax preparation purposes but they're not going to be financial statements that we can rely on for other types of things if necessary like opinion financial statements things like if they want a loan or something like that and this is going to happen typically at some point where a customer is going to want to buy a new house or want to do something like that and they're going to need information on the on the financial statements possibly get a loan for the business. And in order to do that the banks are going to want some more detailed financial statements. And we're not going to provide an opinion as the Bookkeeper.

All we're doing is compiling and entering the data into the system. If we have a CPA firm that we work with then they can typically make any adjustments they need to make more to take our data which is on a cash basis and possibly need to put it on an accrual basis and give their opinion their assurance that the information is in there. So our numbers will be a basis on which that opinion can be made. But we're not going to provide that opinion ourselves for things like an audited financial statement or a reviewed financial statement or some kind of attestation on the financials for things like a loan from the bank whether it be a business loan or a personal loan. And so those will often come up within business needs.

And if we have a CPA firm or an accounting firm, a CPA firm will typically be necessary for an audit or even a review in the US but then that relationship can be really good. And again it's really beneficial because we're not there competing with the CPA firm. Clearly that's where a lot of CPA prints make their money on the review and audit of the attestation type stuff and we can provide the financial data on which that opinion can be built and made. And that's a great relationship to be able to refer people back and forth and work in that kind of format and then payroll is going to be the other item and again payroll can be done by accounting firms and CPA firms.

Note that full service CPA firms however are starting to veer away from accounting for a while now. I'm from payroll because payroll is becoming more specialized it's becoming more so detailed that it's difficult for the CPA firm to do that as well as the other things and probably have higher profit margins in other things like tax preparation and in the attestation like audits and reviews and therefore payrolls becoming something that's becoming kind of a specialty in and of itself. And that's one reason why we as a bookkeeper probably don't we may not want to take on the payroll.

We may want to provide that to someone else unless we are completely reliant on the software like we pay a higher quality software like QuickBooks to do that or we if we're paying for the higher quality software we majors want to export it to someone else to do and that would be the other type of industry we could have and that would be someone like payroll professionals.

The two big ones in the US are ADP and Paychex so ADP is bigger than paychecks. And there's a lot more that could specialize just in payroll. So then again that's a really good networking opportunity that we can then say even with fairly small amounts of payroll if you compare what you would pay for it you almost have to pay some way or another even if we use quick books. We would probably pay for some payroll service. I wouldn't recommend trying to do the manual payroll as the Bookkeeper even if there's only a few customers, even fewer employees and therefore the quits we're going to have to pay someone either we pay for the software or we pay a third party.

And if that's the case it is the Bookkeeper if we want to keep a cash basis system then we might be easier just to simplify that and pay you know a third party and we'll discuss those options as they come into play. Now note again very good relationship here because the payroll professionals these people do just what they do they just do payroll. These are going to be larger companies that also kind of deal with payroll and H.R. kind of issues human resources. So you might find some payroll companies that just do payroll and really specialize on smaller company payroll and might find better value in in that situation as well and that it could be a great relationship note that you can also get a lot of benefits from these relationships meaning you can get referrals they can refer you you can refer them because again you're not competing with them you're helping them any client you get you're helping them. That's a really good relationship.

Also note that you could get paid commissions for these types of things especially for things like payroll. But be very open with that with the customers if you do that if you if you're referring clients to a payroll service and you get paid from them your opinion is no longer you might give a unbiased opinions and still feel that your opinion is it is that is good and it may well be but note that your opinion in appearance at least is not sweetly unbiased now if you're getting paid a commission for the payroll service. So you got it. If you do get paid then it's really you want to be able to present that say hey you know this is who I work with payroll we have a good relationship. They've worked well with me.

I can give you their services. They do provide me a commission on it. Any other one if it's a CPA firm I'd say hey this if they don't give you a commission even say hey this is the CPA firm we have a good relationship they refer me clients I refer them clients we work well together the the cutoffs that we have the system that I put together and how they can pick up the difference between. It works really well but we do have that relationship and you're what you know. So that's just my opinion. You could go to another CPA firm if you want but these are gonna be my opinion. So you want to basically say that you know you do benefit even if you don't get paid. And that's what you would prefer it's probably if you have a certain CPA firm or accounting firm and if you do get paid a commission from something like ADP or Paychex or any kind of payroll and you're referring then be careful and make sure that you're noting that within the discussion just to build trust which is obviously very necessary for any kind of financial services being provided. So other areas to network would be things like financial planning often something that's necessary as of.

So clearly any kind of financial planning whether it be investment planning like a stockbroker or mortgage broker or some kind of financial planner in that format would be useful or debt planning. You know how to reformat debt. Be very careful that you're using reputable people on those types of things. If you have a stockbroker again you know what their fees are on the stock broker. But those are things that you can have referrals if you do get a commission. Be open with any commission on the referrals but those are needs that clients will have and they may ask bookkeepers and whatnot for those types of referrals and it's nice to have some referrals and you may get referrals from them as well insurance agents in other area life insurance health insurance any kind of insurance is another area that you could have other people you want to network with.

Also these are areas that you may take on as a bookkeeper and maybe still not compete with like a CPA firm or Paychex firm. These are areas that you may do bookkeeping and do some financial planning and and be able to pick those up and still be able to differentiate and not be like stepping on the stepping on the toes of the people that are really helping you with your bookkeeping which would probably be the CPA firm and and possibly the payroll.

Real estate agents another one it's going to come up from time to time that you know people are going to want to buy houses and whatnot and that could. So if you know it can refer someone there then that can be useful. Mortgage brokers same thing could be useful as part of oftentimes financial planning and whatnot not just the first time home purchase but financial planning refinancing debt. Oftentimes it's useful to bring in the debt related to the home. And so that could be useful as well.

Bank Feeds Option

Bank feeds as they relate to our proposed cash basis bookkeeping system within cookbooks online. The bank feeds are a great option for a system such as this if we can get access to the bank feeds and download the banking information. It works great in this system because the whole point of this system is Of course to take the information directly from the bank and therefore we don't have the same kind of problems we would use or oftentimes have when downloading bank feeds.

If we're entering the data separately for example if we were entering the data and then we were going to get the data from the bank we could end up with some duplicated information and there's different ways we have to work around that for the bank feeds. In this case we're just getting the data directly from the bank and we're not entering it on our side. We're not entering the information before it clears the bank. We're just getting the information waiting for it to clear and then putting it into the system. Therefore if we can use the bank feed set up this type of system works great for a bank feed set up because it is a cash basis type of system. That said, however , note that the bank fee doesn't solve all the problems that you might think a lot of people think that the bank feeds and they look so great. They are great.

They save a lot of data input time but it's not the case that just having the bank feeds will make it so the whole system just works and the accounting is done for itself through the bank feeds the process that will go through. If we can get access to the bank feeds will be much the same. We'll go through that in a step by step process here. As we enter the data into the system we're going to go through the practice problem here starting out without the bank feeds because that allows you to see what needs to happen whether we use bank feeds or not what the system is actually doing. And then when we set up the bank feeds we're still going to have to set up the system.

In other words it's going to enter the data into the chart of accounts and we're going to have to basically assign that data in a similar way as if we had originally entered the data. The great part of it is however that once we do this a few times the system can memorize many of those transactions and be able then to automate more of those transactions so it will save time. But to just start off with bank feeds is overwhelming because oftentimes we don't know exactly. It's just a lot of data to basically look at and then we have to assign it out. So the same process will apply whether we have the bank feeds or we don't have the bank feeds we'll talk about actually setting up the bank feeds and later chapters we're gonna go through the process however by entering the data and that'll give us directly from the bank statement so we can see exactly what is happening how it goes directly into the register and what we'll have to do on some of those unusual transactions.

Again whether it comes from us manually inputting it into the register or from the bank feeds how can we deal with those transactions. Those are easier to see if we actually go through a month or two entering the data from the bank statement. Also note that to enter the data from the bank feeds will need Of course the banking information from the client so that they will have to have clients that are willing to give us the banking information connect that to the QuickBooks system so that we're working with the cookbook systems that has direct access to the bank feeds. If that's not the case, if we don't have a client that wants to give us the banking information and have it connected to quick books, that's fine. We can still do it from a statement by statement system to get the information on a monthly basis on the bank statements and enter the data for small clients. That's not too difficult to do and it's actually not a bad practice for us to do because then we actually get some familiarity with the vendors.

If we just get the bank feeds especially in the first month we're still gonna have to ask questions like Who are these people. How do I assign this account? I don't know who these vendors are. We got to get a feel for the client and actually entering the data manually can help us to do that and the system will still memorize many of the transactions. So there are some pros and cons with the bank feeds. If we were to have the bank fees the process would be much the same we'd start a new quick books file just like we would if we didn't have the bank feeds we're going to create the chart of accounts using the industry just like we would if we weren't having bank feeds and then we're going to enter transactions each month this time Of course using the bank feeds. That's what the difference would be.

So we'd have to do the same setup process: set up the company file, use the quick books online accountant to manage multiple files if we choose to do so or just enter our personal file. If it's our file then we set up the bank feeds and that allows us to transfer the data directly from the bank into the system and all that information whatever goes through the bank will then just be boom be there. It won't be in the system yet. We'll have to process it through to the system so that's not like the end process especially for the first month. But it saves them data input time.

We'll still need to understand once again how to get that information directly into the bank and assign the proper accounts especially in the first months and that's what we'll learn here. Then we'll do the bank reconciliation process with the bank. Reconciliation doesn't provide the same assurance as if we did the full service bookkeeping because we're relying totally on the bank here. But it does verify that we didn't duplicate the bank fees which is another issue we want to be careful of. Did we download the same feeds twice and have duplicate transactions? Or have we missed some transactions that we didn't download to make sure we have the cutoff dates of when we enter the data correctly within the bank feeds then we'll provide those monthly reports to their clients. So when we start the new company file same process we're gonna need we're going to need to actually purchase a new company file for quick books online we can manage it through our Quickbooks accountant copy we need the name and the industry once set up and that allows us to create the chart of accounts and just move straight forward from there.

Then Of course we'll need the bank feed information which is the banking information will actually be needed to connect to the bank in order to get those bank feeds directly from the bank. We can use our accountants our Quickbooks Online accountant dashboard to manage multiple files if we have multiple files we can have list of multiple files just like we would if we wouldn't have the bank feeds and that'll allow us access to those quick books files we'll create a chart of account based on the industry just like we would if we were not using bank feeds.

Same process here whether we have bank feeds or not we're going to have to assign these charts of accounts to the transactions again whether we use bank feeds or not. And that's gonna be especially for the first couple months no matter what we do we're gonna have to figure that out and assign those out of bank feed or not. And they will enter transactions each month from the bank statement and that's Of course gonna be using the bank feed. So now we'll have the bank feed set up. This is where the same time will be saved rather than us taking the bank statement and entering the data manually.

We just get the bank feed directly from the bank entering the data into our system and then we need to go into that bank feeds all the data that's been put inputs and properly assign it and we have to end that once that happens in the first month that we have to do that in the following months hopefully it'll memorize more and more transactions. But no matter what we do with a new client or if it might be our company file we have to we have the first try to get a feel for what. Then who vendors which vendors are which accounts they need to be assigned to.

How to assign those vendors. Once they've done that. Whether we use bank feeds or not the system will memorize those vendors in some way making the data input for following months much easier. Then we'll do the bank reconciliation just as we would if we didn't have bank feeds. We still need to reconcile why and you might say but I got the data directly from the bank. Why do I need to reconcile it directly from the bank? But note that you can still very easily get devil twice or double up on the amount of data that you downloaded from the bank.

Meaning there's duplicates or miss some of the data on the bank. If you do the bank reconciliation it verifies that that didn't happen. It verifies that you're getting the correct data. So no matter how we enter the data manually from the bank or if we did a full service bookkeeping system we want to do the bank reconciliation is there really something we should do and then we'll provide those reports at the end of the month including the balance sheet the income statement we're going gonna tell the client hey we're still here we're entering the data each month we're gonna be here for you at the end of the year when you need this information most for taxes.

And then we still have those alternative cases that we could use if we had to do bank reconciliations like for example if it was our company file and we're saying hey I needed to enter a year's worth of data. Well we could get multiple months of data from the bank. Now it's limited however. So once we set up the transfers we're gonna have to see how much data we can get from the bank. There are certain limitations but we can certainly use the bank feeds to get as much information as possible so that we can enter if we had to enter a year's worth of data and then we'll have to basically assign that.

Now once again note if you take on a job whether it be your client whether be your company file or clients and you're going to enter a year's worth of data or even in multiple months worth of data and just download it from the bank as you download the data it's gonna be a huge just compile of data a mess that you're going to have then we'll still have to go through each of those transactions and assign them out because the system won't have memorized the transactions yet and won't know where they go. So just be aware that the bank reconciliations or the banking connection downloading the bank feeds directly for an entire year's worth of information will be an overwhelming process.

If you're not used to the bank feeds and no matter what we do we're still gonna have to go through line by line for a while and make sure that we assign the proper accounts until the system can memorize and help us out to assign more accounts out. So we'll talk a bit more about the best way to do that is basically to practice a few times entering the data directly from a bank statement. One transaction at a time so we can actually see you know one transaction at a time and see where it goes rather than just kind of being overwhelmed with a huge set of data and then trying to go through it line by line and when we're probably feeling a little bit overwhelmed at that point so we'll do it one month at a time here and we'll start off and see how that is done and then see how the bank feeds can shorten or ease that process.

Once we get it set up and then we'll do the bank reconciliations for multiple months and then we would provide the monthly reports for multiple months if we had to do multiple months at one time. Same process bank feeds or no. Note that Of course the client has access to the files no matter what the same process is. We might have the quick books accountant and we get access to the file.

We can have that the client can go into the file as well. Our same scenario would be that the client has access if they want to leave so that they can get the data. It's not our data. We're not trying to hoard the file on our side. We're just trying but we are trying to separate the data input so that we just get the bank feeds. We enter the data so that only one person is entering the data so that we know exactly what's happening. That should be the easiest way to keep the data clean. And then a client has access to the file to print reports. We can also provide that file to tax preparers or whoever necessary at the end of the year.

Engagement Letter and Questionnaire

Within the engagement letter and a questionnaire chapter of the Book will go over some common practices, some best practices for setting the engagements, the terms of the engagement with a bookkeeping firm and a business. This is important even if we're doing our own bookkeeping even if we're setting this system up as the owner of a business because it helps us to define the different terms of different segments that can be subdivided whether we do it ourselves or others and if we are a bookkeeper we want to know the best practices of the engagement as well so that we can clearly define the thing that we are doing and the things that we are not doing because what we're not doing.

Defining those items is just as important as what we are doing because once we define those then we can network based on those skills based on what we are doing. We want to be very definite with that and we also want to be very clear with the client so they know what is expected from us and what is not expected. If we do our own bookkeeping we want to know what is standard with our bookkeeping as opposed to say year end type of information tax preparation information financial statement information when we have a client and a business relationship between a bookkeeping firm and a client.

One way to do that is to have the engagement letter. The engagement letter will clearly define this is what we think. This is what should happen on the business side. This is the information we will need and this is what we do on the bookkeeping side and it'll define what we don't do.

What we don't do is what the limits of the type Of course we keep are and therefore the book. When the client needs other services that are kind of related like tax preparation or other items. Then Of course we can look at that on a field by field basis and clearly define the terms and not have that kind of job creep that comes up also. Which means that we'll have added work that's done without that's not clearly defined in the contract.

We want the thing to be clearly defined so everybody involved just like any kind of business arrangement knows everything. Everything is transparent as best as possible and then we have the questionnaire. A questionnaire is going to be something we want to ask the client to make sure that we can set up our business model as best we can to fit their needs as best we can. So we're gonna be doing a cash based system.

We want to ask questions to make sure that what the client has is something that fits into our system so that we can see and be very clear again upfront and say that you fit well into the system we have perfect. If it doesn't fit well into the system will say hey there's some areas where things don't quite fit. Not quite a perfect match but we have some workarounds of that and we want to be clear and upfront with that. The questionnaire will help us to kind of define those types of items.

Engagement Letter

In this chapter we will discuss the pros and cons of an engagement letter. A more formal contract between the bookkeeper and the client. This is useful information whether we are a bookkeeper or whether we are looking for services for financial services tax preparation bookkeeping services because this will allow us a format and think about how we want to define what we are looking for from that contract from that engagement.

So an engagement letter has the goals of defining what we are responsible for. So if we're the bookkeeper What is it that we are responsible for and implicitly that's going to define what we are not responsible for. We're also going to say explicitly some of the things that we are not responsible for and this is really important because a lot of times the client doesn't really have an idea of what we are doing and what we're not doing an informal contract if we just say hey we're doing the bookkeeping and we get paid for the bookkeeping there's still a contract there we still have a contractual agreement and all the elements of a normal contract are present. However that contract is not very defined.

We don't know exactly what the rules are of that contract. We haven't formally put it down in writing. The more defined the contract is the easier it will be able to do especially if we're trying to differentiate the things that we do as a bookkeeper and trying to work with other individuals such as a tax preparation or such as payroll and define what it is that we do and what we would like to outsource and work with other professionals to do in that capacity. So that's really helpful to make those definitions that we want.

We want to do that formally with a letter if possible so an engagement letter In other words not required because we can't have a formal contract or we can't have an informal contract. A verbal contract is an agreement through just a handshake and an agreement and the performance of work. However a formal contract such as an engagement letter in order to list out what we do and what the others are responsible for is very useful. That being the other format, the other necessary or the other component of an engagement letter that's going to say what the client is responsible for. So it's gonna say what we do and it's going to say what the client does and be as specific as possible in those terms. It's also going to reduce liability for us or that's a hope in that we're going to define what by defining what we are responsible for.

We're limiting the responsibility about those things that we are not responsible for. So there shouldn't be any confusion about the things that we're not covering under this engagement and therefore we should have less liability about problems related to those particular things. It's also going to reduce job creep which is basically a concept that once you start working. It's often the case where the job, the components of the job or the things that the client wants done seems to increase over time. And oftentimes that happens and we don't really understand. We don't really pick it up in the billing. We're not being very specific on what we do and what we do not do. And therefore as the increased desires of the client increase we're not picking it up in the billing and we can also mess up basically our system.

Basically I go into systems that are outside the design of what we do and so we want to be very specific on what we do because that's how we specialize and if we start to have job creep and we start to differentiate in the things that we do we may find ourselves doing work that is less efficient and not basically being as efficient being able to help as many people and be able to be as profitable. It's also just a goal to keep everyone happy through understanding and you would think that an engagement letter because it's a formal thing that would reduce or make make it could make a relationship more difficult but in a business relationship it typically in many kind of relationships it will it will make it easier because it's going to define the terms what we're looking for what the other person wants.

It makes more transparency in the negotiation which within business is going to be really useful. We want transparency. We want to know what each party thinks about the engagement or thinks they want from the engagement and be very clear about those things and then we can actually measure whether or not either party is providing those things. So although we're doing the bookkeeping service Book there our response goes on both sides in order for the engagement to work and the more transparent we can make those things the better.

And this was supposed to indicate that there's a meeting of the minds which is often the terminology that is used within contracts a meeting of the minds of mutual agreement and understanding between two individuals and that's often what basically a contract is going to be defined as in the most transparent more more transparent that is the better the meeting of the minds is. So they're not like headbutting here, that's a meeting, that's meeting of the minds. So here's an engagement letter now. I don't typically add a lot of detail in terms of just writing for a PowerPoint slide.

I've given it an example of the Engage letter so you can take a look at it. But I think it's useful to go through some of the terms and note this is just an example of an engagement letter you can make. Any format you want and refine it down but just look at some examples of just a stock engagement letter for a bookkeeping type of business. So this letter is to confirm our space and specify the terms of our engagement with you and to clarify the nature and extent of services we will provide. We will perform the following services for you each. Whatever it's going to be month quarter what not from the list below we're gonna choose the list items down here.

Typically our system I'm just listed out what I would recommend that we're talking about here. These services will begin whenever they're gonna begin and we might want to update this engagement letter from time to time as well. Notice that agreements will change over time. We have an agreement with people that it's okay for those things to change but as things change if we start to see job creep happening if we're happy with more work then that's good. But we should then recap our engagement letter.

Make sure that they're defined from time to time. So we're going to record cash receipts income from your bank statements. We're gonna record cash disbursements expense expenses from what should be your bank statement. We're gonna reconcile bank accounts and we're going to provide financial reports including profit loss report and balance sheet on a cash basis. Note that these reports are not reviewed or audited financial statements and we're gonna provide a backup file of your financial data if and when requested.

So those are just gonna be the simplified bookkeeping terms again and we could reword that make it a little bit nicer in terms of the wording we do want to make it kind of lawyerly type of wording and define for example that the financial statements are not issuing an opinion and be clear about something like that and define what we're doing on this next paragraph. Our engagement is limited to the period and accounting services indicated above. So we had the starting period. If we don't have a set ending period we're going to want to put the set ending period if it's going to be a continuing engagement then we might want to mention that it's going to be continuing until such a point that either party can terminate the engagement for whatever reason that they want.

Basically we will not audit or review your financial statements so that's important that we're not doing. An opinion is what that means as those terms are defined and generally accepted auditing standards or any other accounting documents and information you provide. We will not verify the data you submit for accuracy or completeness. So and this seems like we're trying to kind of get out of what we're trying to do here but that's if we need to be specific on that. Our goal is not that we're not trying to audit or give an opinion and we have to be specific on that because those are specific terms within financial statements and so we're not. We want to make sure that we're not giving some indication because we've entered the data that it's assured.

So and a lot of times customers will actually ask us for things like that if they might ask us for example if we're making deductions that they think our business or personal and start to ask us and start to tell us well and argue why it would be a personal or why it should be a business expense because that would lower their income taxes and we have to note that hey you know we're not doing the tax preparation we're entering the data that you provide for us we were going to ask or think that you should go to the tax professional for that if you tell us that's something that is deductible or is part of a business expense as opposed to a personal.

We're pretty much going to go by the information that you have here and we're going to recommend it. And that doesn't mean that you should feel comfortable with the IRS necessarily. It may be good or maybe not. You know if you want that kind of opinion then you've got to go to the tax office to give you that kind of assurance because they're the one that's going to have to argue the case if there's any issue there. So we want to be clear on those types of things. Rather we will rely on the accuracy and completeness of the documents and information you provide to us. You are responsible for designing and implementing controls. So note that we're saying what the other party is responsible for as well here. So it's not just our terms that we're looking at.

This isn't just what we're going to do, we're going to this is a mutual agreement between the two of us to prevent and detect fraud and inform us about all known or suspected fraud impacting the company. So basically we're basically saying hey we're not. You're the one you're responsible for internal controls basically to detect fraud. Our services here in entering data aren't designed to detect financial statement fraud. We're entering data. In addition you are responsible for identifying and ensuring that the entity complies with applicable laws and regulations. So again we're basically saying that it's your responsibility to apply it to comply with laws, not our responsible ability as the bookkeeper to make sure that the company is doing so.

So we're not taking on that responsibility that's the responsibility Of course of the business in order for us to complete this engagement in a timely and efficient manner we request access to documents concerning your financial transactions including but not limited to bank statements canceled checks credit card statements and any other financial information necessary that impacts our accounting records. Now this seems obvious but clearly we need to. We need to indicate this. If we haven't completed the job Of course then the question is why haven't we done our end of the job or have we not been able to.

Based on the fact that we don't have all the information such as the financial information so we want to be clear on what is needed for us to finish up the job. Our fee for these services will be based upon the amount of time requested at our standard billing rate plus out-of-pocket expenses. Now this fee may differ. I'm not going to get into fees here on what type of fees you could have. We might have a fixed fee. We might have a fee just based on the number of transactions which for small companies is pretty good.

We could say hey how many transactions do you have for a company that has that many transactions. That's a complete bookkeeping based company. This is what we charge. And then if they go up to the next level of number of transactions we can up our fees so we may not have just a fee. In other words based on just time spent. That's just kind of the default if we don't have any other kind of form that you may want to think of a format of saying hey if you only have this many transactions in one bank account and we're not doing payroll or anything else then this is the fee. If your transactions go above this level this is the fee.

If you want to tack on payroll if you want to take on payroll or some other type of information charge a flat fee because that kind of thing will be easier to discuss in some cases. But we won't get into the fees here. Just note whatever your fee terms are, we can put that in the engagement letter. All invoices are due and payable upon chapter. Our maximum liability to you arises for any reasons related to services rendered under this letter shall be limited to the amount of fees you paid for these services. So again this is our attempt to limit our liability. We're going to hear our maximum liabilities that we charged you here.

We're agreeing to that. We don't want to get sued for that and that may not stop a lawsuit. Above that in some cases you know it doesn't mean it'll completely stop a lawsuit but that's the agreement we're coming to hear. That's the agreement. We want to be at. And that is that we're limited to our fees. What we've collected from you in the event of a claim of third party related or services under this letter you will indemnify us from all such claims, liabilities , costs and expenses except to the extent determined to have resulted from our intentional or deliberate misconduct. So again we're attempting to limit our liability exposure here to at least our fees if any dispute arises between the parties here to the part the parties agree first to try in good faith to settle the dispute through non-binding mediation.

Now this is an attempt and we could include this or we may not but we notice that are our goals. If there is a dispute is to basically sue somebody which is to go through the normal court process or to have some other type of mediation a normal lawsuit is usually really expensive for all involved because you have to hire lawyers and go through the entire process mediation or some other type of process is usually less costly. So we're trying to say here this is basically saying hey if there is a problem let's try. Let's try to work it out. Let's try to talk about it.

Let's unless we can get a mediator which will be someone that can mediate which will help us to have a third party to talk to each other. Let's not just go into our separate corners, get a lawyer and not talk to each other. All right. And now try to work it out. So this is an attempt to try to discuss what type of dispute resolution we will have if there is an event in the future of a problem the cost of mediation shall be shared equally by the parties. And again mediation does mean that we're going to look for somebody but it's not a formal process to go to court it's going to be mediated which usually requires some other person that's going to be assigned as kind of a go between a negotiator between the disputed parties.

So the parties agree if any dispute cannot be set off through mediation the dispute may then be brought before a court of competent jurisdiction. But the battle. But the matter will ultimately be decided by the court sitting without a jury. So again we're trying to avoid the costly ness of the jury. So the parties recognize they have knowingly and voluntarily agreed to waive all rights to have any such dispute determined by a jury but otherwise retain all rights afforded under the applicable civil justice system.

So again you may not have all this kind of stuff but it's trying to limit the type of the type of legal costs that we have. It doesn't mean you can't go through legal problems. It's just how you are going to go through the legal dispute. Do we want to? We want to avoid that. The most costly way which is to to go through the normal jury kind of process and the least costly way would have to have mediation and if mediation doesn't work because it's not totally binding then we're looking for some other format that we can settle our differences through the legal system without a full fledged jury trial.

New Client Engagement Questionnaire

In this chapter we will discuss a new client engagement questionnaire, a list of questions that we can ask when assessing whether or not we want to take on or work with a new client. These are also questions that we can ask ourselves if we're thinking about setting up a system for our own bookkeeping system. We do have a copy of the questionnaire so you can take a look at the questionnaire and print it out and use it adjusted to whatever your needs are.

For a questionnaire to jot down your needs for a specific client or for the bookkeeping system. This is gonna be a couple of questions that we want to go through. If we could imagine ourselves in an interview process thinking about whether we want to take on an engagement with ourselves and a new potential client. So some of the questions we might ask are: What type of industry are you in? And that'll give us an idea if it's going to be related to industries that we have worked with in the past.

Also give us an idea of the things that we want to watch out for and that's going to be things like does that industry involve inventory. Because that's one of those things that we want to be more sure on whether or not we want to take on inventory related customers or not. And there may be other things that are industry related that will help us to determine whether or not our bookkeeping system will be useful for that particular industry. And we'll get more specific questions related to those needs as well. Is it a new business or a continuing business or is this business starting from scratch.

Is this going to be the first year of operations or do we have a continuing business. It's okay either way if we have the continuing business. We can't still enter the books as of this point in time going forward but then our needs Of course may differ in terms of what is that prior information and we may have questions and look for information about how the prior business has been doing possibly how the prior bookkeeper was what was the prior bookkeeping system and why has it changed. We may ask the primary reason for a bookkeeping service.

What are they looking for? And normally if we're applying this system were usually looking for a smaller bookkeeper so there may be a need we probably know is going to be compiling data for a year in tax preparation. Probably one of the major reasons that you're going to have the information they want. They want to compile the information for taxes typically is what we were assuming to to have one of their main needs and possibly Of course for internal use as well just confidence that they're recording their information having financial information which is somewhat reliable. The other thing we could ask is the type of entity that they are meaning are they a sole proprietor.

Are we a partnership or a general partnership or a Limited Liability Company an S corporation or a C Corporation. Now we're expecting Of course most of our clients to be sole proprietors. That's what we're kind of gearing towards with this cash basis type of system. If there is a C Corporation a normal corporation that usually means that they're larger in nature.

Most C Corporations are larger now doesn't necessarily need to be the case. So if it's a small C corporation for whatever reason they wanted to be a C corporation and they still have a very few transactions then we may want to take that down. But if they're a C corporation we would probably be more suspicious that it would be a larger level and they may need more than we can provide in terms of the types Of Book Keeping that they're looking for.

Our bookkeeping is geared towards a limited number of cash based systems. If they're a partnership they could be fairly small and still be a partnership and we could take on a partnership as well however we need the added. We have the added problem of them being partners in tracking the capital accounts. So if they are a partnership we probably want to make sure that we are working with a CPA firm in order to to allocate the net income properly between the capital accounts so that the two partners have that allocation. So we may have one more level of assurance that we might want to do above and beyond just entering the data for the net income at the end of the time period compiling that data. So if there is a corporation it's possible to have a single member even as Corporation a very small corporation. So if that's the case we don't have to be too intimidated by that.

It's possible to have a small customer that has the S corporation's probably less common for this type of client that we're looking for. If they have an S corporation and we might think maybe they're larger than what we're doing but it's but it's possible they're not because they might have other reasons for an S corporation. So we the type of interest in the type of entity could give us some idea and we're talking here basically tax identity.

So these are going to be tax identity, how they're going to file their taxes is one where we can consider these types of entities we would expect the sole proprietor who is responsible for financial reporting and taxes.

Now again if it's a sole proprietor we would expect to be talking to that individual because they're probably the ones talking to us if we have a larger industry or for there's a few people involved then we want to know specifically who it is that we should be going to. That's the ultimate leave responsible within your organization for this information for the financial information so that we know who they go to. Again typically for smaller companies. We would be talking to that individual hopefully to see if we want to set up an engagement such as this. Have you worked with other bookkeepers in the past? So we want to see if there is a continuing engagement.

How have you done your books in the past? How have you done your taxes in the past? Who? Who do you work with? Who have you worked with in the past? What's your system there? And with relation to that if you have then who were they. If you would be willing to give us some information. What. Most times people are because there's a reason why they stopped. Whatever system they have whether it wasn't working for them whether they thought you know there is some problem with the people that were putting it together the system just wasn't given the right information.

What services were provided by the prior bookkeeper did they do for bookkeeping service. Did they do just a partial, did they just kind of compile things together at the end of the year for taxes or how do you know how. How did this work in the prior bookkeeping system? What were your likes and dislikes? Did you like the bookkeeping system? What were the things that are making you change in essence from one bookkeeping system to another. And may we contact them if it is a bookkeeper or another CPA firm or someone else was compiling ? It's useful for us to contact them.

I mean because we can then get a relationship and we might need data for ourselves possibly for our bookkeeping but possibly also if we if we try to recommend some other things such as tax preparation or financial statement preparation then those things oftentimes are necessary for us to have some of the prior data in order to compile those it may be for taxes we may not need them for tax if it's a small company going forward because really we oftentimes just need the profit loss the activity throughout the time period which we can put together but we may need meet needs some other information. And it's also useful just to ask the other bookkeeping firm what the client was like. Is it OK if we ask them you know did you get along with the client where they go.

Do they pay you on time for those kinds of things? So if we're, it's OK for us to ask the other bookkeeper and contact them. Often a useful thing because we want to be careful on who we start doing the bookkeeping work with because clients that are difficult could take a lot of time and result in not being worth the payment. We can be in situations where we are not getting paid and putting in a lot of work. So we want to be. We want to be careful on that and if we can contact any prior bookkeeper that could be useful in that regard as well. Does your business have inventory now? That's going to be one of these areas that our system that we're discussing here is going to be one in which inventory is something we would probably want to stay away from most of the time.

We're going to give an example problem with inventory so you can see how to work around it. If we picked up clients with inventory but what we're not doing is giving a full service inventory tracking we're not going to track the service inventory within quick books under that system. And therefore if that's what the client wants we're going to set something else up now we'll discuss some ways to take on. Take a look at the inventory in your question for yourself.

Here would be then do I want to take on a customer that has inventory or not do I just want to look for customers do I want to specialize in the customers that are just service companies and there's a lot of those out there and companies that I don't need to deal with the inventory for and if you do deal with inventory then how can we how can we set up a system what type of customers do we want you know. And for those inventory needs we still have some limitations in terms of how much inventory information we can deal with or how we can deal with customers and clients with inventory. Do you have employees in other words do you have a need for payroll. That's another area that oftentimes we don't really want to take on internally we're going to argue here not to take on the payroll internally.

It's possible to do that with QuickBooks and pay for the full service payroll. But doing that is really you're still paying someone for the payroll to set up the payroll and it's going to make the system a bit more complex. It's not completely a cash basis or not information was taken directly from the bank statement. So we're going to argue that if there are employees then that's OK. But how are you dealing with those employees? Have you been paying them with a third party who's been processing your payroll before this.

Because again it has to have some kind of payroll process if it's an ongoing business because payroll is complex and even if it's only one or two employees there's going to have to be some withholdings there is going to be some process for making that formation happen. So if they don't have payroll and this could be our question once again if if they do we want to take on customers that maybe just don't have payroll just small sole proprietor companies sole proprietor not company sole proprietor businesses that don't have payroll and not have to deal with that at all or take on customers and work with a payroll company to to allow that payroll company to work with payroll or maybe even try to take on payroll by paying for the payroll service within Quick Books which is something we're not really recommended here.

We're basically saying this simplified system takes on the customers that don't have payroll or customers for which you can help them get a third party payroll individual for what banking institution you use. So we want to make sure that we know the banking institution so that we can get the financial statements from the banking institution. We want to basically note that they have no banking institution for which we can get the financial statements from. Do you have a separate business checking account? Hopefully they have a separate business checking account that's going to make it a lot easier because our whole system is based on the separate business checking account. If they do not, if they're mixing their personal and business accounts then things get a lot more messy. We can still deal with that but it's going to be a lot uglier for us to do.

We're going to take their account and we're gonna enter it into our system and we're going to have to then differentiate and figure out what is a personal expense or a business expense. And so sometimes it's possible to do that if it's a small company. We can go in there and we can try to ferret out and separate the two and call one a draw and the other expenses but it's a lot more difficult. So if the company doesn't have a separate bank account for the business we would suggest doing so because that's how our system is set up. We're assuming that everything that goes into the bank for the business checking account is business related. And if that's the case then. But then the bank is really doing the bookkeeping for us and all we really have to do is take that data and reformat it into the proper categories.

If on the other hand we're talking about a checking account that has business and personal then our work has gotten a lot more difficult because now we don't know where were the whether these transactions should be business or personal we can't come up with that pre assumption that for example all deposits we would think would be from a customer it was a checking account for a business but if it's a personal checking account maybe maybe they're getting money from other sources that aren't business related and that really muddies the water up in terms of how are we going to separate out the data. So if they don't have a separate checking account we would really want to set up a separate checking account typically if you have a business credit card or business credit card.

Another area that really kind of muddies the water is if they don't use business credit cards and they just use the checking account then that's basically easier because we have a business checking their credit cards if they use them. Are they separating the credit cards for their business from personal gain if they're using one credit card for business and personal purposes? That gets messy. We would at least recommend having two credit cards if they do use credit cards. We have a question of whether we want to. Do we want to take on clients that have credit cards? We have to sort out what we want to set up a system that we're not sorting out the credit cards and that they do that outside the system or we do that or something outside the system.

We can also ask whether or not they pay off their credit cards every month or have an outstanding balance on the business credit card because that makes a difference in terms of tracking it if they pay it off every month. Then we know that the amount that they paid the amount that hit the bank statement is for those transactions on the credit card. If they paid if they paid off only part of it. Now we have this loan as liability which is kind of accrual accounting. So if they're dealing with business credit cards it adds a level of complication. We'll discuss how to deal with that and a couple of different options we can deal with credit cards as well.

But that's something that we want to know about upfront and know about whether or not or how the client would like to be dealing with the credit cards. How can we transfer data each month? Now each month we're gonna need at a minimum a bank statement from the customer and possibly the credit card statement. So we need those two things and then we're going to enter the data and then we're going to provide back to the client the customer the financial statements each month and or a backup file of the QuickBooks data. So we need to know how we are going to do that. And there's multiple different ways Of course that can happen.

We can always go by just mail. We can use email if we're not comfortable with e-mail there's different ways that we would want to format the email to make sure that it's secure and whatnot if we're not comfortable with e-mail that there's other kinds of formats we can use including cloud based formats like a Google Drive or. Or the dropbox. Different kinds of ways that we can store on the cloud that can be more secure. We're looking for a secure way to give and receive the documents. Obviously the files that are given in terms if it's just a PDA file for the bank statements and we're giving back PDA files then the size of the files are pretty small so we can probably get free.

Google Drive or free Dropbox. And the email wouldn't be too large to email those types of files. However if we are providing backup for and that's one of the benefits of the system is that we don't have to trade backup files which are larger. We're just basically giving back and forth documentation which is typically pretty small so we can do that over basically any distance we can do that if we can find pretty secure ways to do that. If however we're giving and receiving PD backup files for quick books then that gets a little bit more difficult if we give the backup file back then we're gonna have to give that back in some format that's large enough to be able to store that much data.

Again it's probably possible on a google drive but if we have multiple clients and we do that a lot then we're probably going to have to pay at some point for the storage space for that kind of system. If we're just giving documentation and we're only giving the backup file as requests and when needed or periodically then we can probably set up even a cloud based system for free basically and be able to go through that process. But whatever the process is, we want to make sure that both the client and us are comfortable with it from a security basis and from just a logistics basis. How are we going to do this to make it as easy as possible?